Shooting Star
Annie Oakley, the Legend

Debbie Dadey
Illustrations by Scott Goto

Walker and Company
New York

First published in the United States of America in 1997 by Walker Publishing Company, Inc.; first paperback edition published in 1999

Published simultaneously in Canada by Thomas Allen & Son Canada, Limited, Markham, Ontario

Library of Congress Cataloging-in-Publication Data
Dadey, Debbie.
Shooting star: Annie Oakley, the legend/Debbie Dadey: illustrations by Scott Goto.
p. cm.
Summary: An exaggerated account of the life and exploits of the sharp-shooting entertainer.
ISBN 0-8027-8484-4 (hardcover). —ISBN 0-8027-8485-2 (reinforced)
1. Oakley, Annie, 1860–1926—Juvenile literature. 2. Shooters of firearms—United States—Biography—Juvenile
literature. 3. Women entertainers—United States—Biography—Juvenile literature. [1. Oakley, Annie, 1860–1926.
2. Sharpshooters. 3. Entertainers. 4. Women—Biography.] I. Goto, Scott, ill. II. Title.
GV1157.03D33   1997
796.3 092—dc20
[B]
ISBN 0-8027-7559-4 (paperback)

96–24821
CIP
AC

The illustrations in this book were painted with acrylic and oil on Bristol paper.

Book design by Krystyna Skalski

Printed in Hong Kong
2 4 6 8 10 9 7 5 3

For Father William Allard, a real star in the world.
With special thanks to Jeanne Gardner,
who shares in my respect and admiration for Annie Oakley.
—D. D.

Thanks to my family and friends, Debbie Dadey,
Emily Easton, and everyone at Walker and Company.
—S. G.

Ping! Ping! Ping!

"Pa! She's at it again!" Annie Oakley's ma shook her head. "Why can't she play with a rattle like most babies?"

"Annie ain't like most babies." Pa rubbed his whiskers and watched.

One-year-old Annie was spitting bullets out of her cradle. *Ping! Ping!* Annie hit the tin roof of the family barn.

"Annie." Pa patted her head. "You've got to stop this. You're driving the cows plumb loco."

Annie did try, but every once in a while she'd forget, like babies tend to do. *Ping! Ping! Ping!*

Pa ended up moving the barn fifteen miles down the road just to keep Annie from spitting bullets at it.

Now back in those days, folks either grew their supper or shot it. When Annie's pa up and died, someone needed to help Ma out. Annie didn't have much of a green thumb, so when she was five, she started hunting game for the cooking pot.

"Annie," Ma said, "what would we do without the food you bring home?"

"Aw, Ma," Annie said, kicking her toe into the cabin's dirt floor. "I just want to help."

Fact was, Annie liked a challenge as much as she liked helping. She didn't just shoot at the game she was hunting. "Yee-haw!" she'd yell, twirling around three times, doing a flip, and then shooting.

Annie even paid for the family farm by selling meat in town. "Dang it all," the store-keeper told Annie, "you're the best durn shot around. You ought to try your luck at this shooting match."

Annie looked at the flyer hanging on the wall. It offered a hundred dollars to anyone who could outshoot the great Frank Butler. "Yee-haw!" Annie hollered. "I'll do it!"

FRANK BUTLER

Annie's hands shook a bit, but she did love a challenge. So off she went to the shooting match. A lot of people guffawed when little fifteen-year-old Annie stepped up to shoot against the world-famous marksman. When she hit every target, their eyeballs just about popped out onto the ground.

Word was that Frank Butler lost something more valuable than a hundred dollars that day: He lost his heart. In a few years Annie and Frank got hitched and took up with Buffalo Bill's Wild West Show.

Annie was the show's star trick shooter. She practiced hard and, before long, people came from hundreds of miles just to see her put out a candle with one bullet, shoot out the center of a playing card, or knock a dime from Frank's fingers.

"Missy," Frank told Annie one day after a show, "You can out-shoot any man or woman in the whole American West."

Buffalo Bill slapped Annie on the back. "Why stop with this country? I'm taking the Wild West Show to Europe. Will you go?"

Annie nodded. "Sure, I just want to help."

"Bon voyage!" shouted hundreds of well-wishers as the Wild West Show loaded bears, elk, deer, mules, sixteen buffalo, and a hundred and sixty horses onto the steamship *State of Nebraska*.

Sure enough, when they got to Europe, all kinds of royal folks came to see Annie. Her hands shook a bit when she saw Queen Victoria watching her. But did Annie miss a shot? Not Annie!

"You are a very clever girl," the Queen said when Annie visited the palace. Annie smiled and curtsied. It was hard for her to believe she'd once worried about having enough to eat, and now here she was jawing with royalty.

The Grand Duke Michael of Russia didn't think Annie was so clever. He liked to think he was the best marksman in the world, so he challenged Annie to a shooting match.

Ping! Ping! Ping! The Grand Duke hit thirty-five out of fifty targets. No one said a word when Annie stepped up to shoot. Annie's hands shook a bit before she lifted the gun. Was she good enough to beat the best marksman in Russia?

Ping! Ping! Ping! She hit forty-seven targets and became the best sharpshooter not only in the American West but in the whole world.

When Annie returned to America, the great Sioux Indian chief Sitting Bull joined the Wild West Show. The audience would boo whenever Sitting Bull entered the show. Because of the wars between the settlers and the Indians, they thought Sitting Bull was plumb mean. Annie saw right away that they were wrong. She visited Sitting Bull's tent often and chatted with him.

One evening Sitting Bull looked at Annie, and then pointed to the starry sky. "You are the best sharpshooter in the world. Tonight, I give you a bigger challenge. Can you shoot the point off a star with my old gun?"

Annie never liked to back down from a challenge. "I reckon I could give it a try," she told Sitting Bull.

The Times
OAKLEY TO SHOOT STAR

The next day she started practicing. She poured a wagonload of powder into her rifle and packed it tight with a broom handle. With a steady hand, Annie lifted her gun and aimed. *Ping! Ping! Ping!* Annie made three craters in the moon.

"I reckon I'm ready," Annie said. She chose a star fifteen million light-years away and loaded her gun. People gathered from all over the world to watch her. If she could make this shot, she would be the greatest sharpshooter in the universe.

Annie used two wagonloads of gunpowder, tapped it in tightly with a tree limb, and lifted the gun to her shoulder.

Before

After

The explosion was so loud it caused the Snake River to flow backward and it shucked corn in fifteen states. When the smoke cleared, Sitting Bull let out a shout that could be heard in Paris, France. The crowd cheered so hard they turned Annie's hair pure white.

"You did it!" Frank yelled. Annie nodded and smiled. She had shot not one point but all five points off the star. One point landed smack dab in the middle of Colorado. Folks later named it Pike's Peak. Three points broke into pieces in the Pacific Ocean, creating the Hawaiian Islands. Annie plucked up the smallest point and stuck it on her hat for decoration.

Annie Oakley had faced her biggest challenge. She was now the greatest sharpshooter in the universe.

Sitting Bull put his hand on Annie's shoulder. "Will you be my adopted daughter? I will call you Little Sureshot."

"I'd be plumb proud," Annie told Sitting Bull. So they had the ceremony right then and there. Annie Oakley became an official Sioux that day.

Now you know that Annie was tickled to jelly to be the best sharpshooter in the universe *and* a Sioux, but she never let success go to her head.

"Lands a mercy," Annie told Frank years later. "I have more gold medals than a hive has bees." She pointed to their wagon train. Every wagon was loaded down with medals and awards that Annie had won.

"I think it's time we did some helping," Annie said. She hauled off all those gold medals, melted them down, and sold the gold. She gave the money to a hospital for poor children.

"Yippee for Annie Oakley!" the children cheered.

"Aw, shucks," Annie said. "I just wanted to help." Annie was famous the world over, but she never forgot what it had been like to be poor when she was a child.

Annie never retired. She just kept shooting until one day she up and died. They buried her with a gun in her hand, and some folks say that she's still doing what she loves best.

Maybe you've seen her. Every time you see a shooting star in the sky, that's just Annie Oakley facing another challenge.

THE TRUTH

Annie Oakley was born in Darke County, Ohio, in 1860 and was the best sharpshooter this country has ever known.

The truth is that Annie really did pay off the debts of her family's farm by selling meat when she was about thirteen. She also beat Frank Butler in a shooting match.

She married Frank Butler and really shot dimes from his fingers, ashes off his cigarette, and holes in his playing cards. She was an amazing woman who could even shoot out candle flames.

She did beat a Russian Grand Duke in a shooting match and was Sitting Bull's adopted daughter. Later in life, Annie Oakley, whose real name was Phoebe Ann Mosey (*Moses* in some sources), cared enough to melt her gold medals, sell them, and give the money to a hospital.

Annie Oakley, who always practiced gun safety, is a larger-than-life legend of the Old West. Much has been written about her, some truth and some exaggeration. *Shooting Star* is mostly exaggeration, but the truth is that Annie Oakley really was a shooting star.